MACHINE LEARNING APPROACHES IN NEURO-LOGICAL DISORDER DIAGNOSIS

Submitted by

        Manohar   Chaudhary, Chandigarh University
Mr.   Jayesh   Surana   ,Chandigarh University

TABLE OF CONTENTS

ABSTRACT 5
CHAPTER 1 6
INTRODUCTION 6
    1.1.   Client Identification/Need Identification/Identification of relevant Contemporary issue 6
    1.2.   Identification of Problem 8
    1.3.   Identification of Tasks 10
    1.4.   Timeline 13
    1.5.   Organization of the Report 14
CHAPTER 2 17
LITERATURE REVIEW / BACKGROUND STUDY 17
    2.1   Timeline of the Reported Problem 17
    2.2.   Existing Solutions 19
    2.3.   Bibliometric analysis 20
    2.4.   Review Summary 22
    2.5.   Problem Definition 23
    2.6.   Goals/ Objective 24
CHAPTER 3 27
DESIGN/FLOW PROCESS 27
    3.1   Evaluation & Selection of Specifications/Features 27

3.2 Design Constraints:	29
3.3 Analysis of Features and finalization subject to constraints	31
3.4 Design Flow	32
3.5 Design Selection:	35
3.6 Implementation Plan/Methodology	37
CHAPTER 4	**40**
RESULTS ANALYSIS AND VALIDATION	**40**
4.1 Implementation of solution	40
CHAPTER 5	**44**
CONCLUTION AND FUTURE SCOPE	**44**
5.1 Conclusion :	44
5.2 Future Scope :	45
REFRENCES	**48**

ABSTRACT

Brain stroke is a critical medical condition characterized by the disruption of blood circulation in the brain, leading to severe damage and potential disabilities. With worldwide implications as the second leading cause of death and third leading cause of disability, early diagnosis and preventive measures are crucial. This project leverages machine learning techniques to develop a robust diagnostic model for predicting the likelihood of a stroke based on patient data. The dataset encompasses various demographic and health-related attributes, including age, gender, hypertension, heart disease, marital status, occupation, residence type, average glucose level, BMI, smoking status, and the occurrence of a stroke. The machine learning models employed include Logistic Regression, Naive Bayes, Support Vector Machine (SVM), and K Nearest Neighbors (KNN). Following these traditional models, a neural network architecture was implemented, achieving an impressive accuracy of 95%. The dataset was preprocessed through standardization, and a train-validation split ratio of 80:20 was adopted. The project's primary objective is to identify the most accurate predictive model among the tested algorithms. The findings will contribute to enhancing stroke prediction accuracy and, consequently, aid in timely intervention and prevention strategies. The subsequent chapters of this project will delve into the methodology, data preprocessing, model development, and results analysis. By understanding the intricacies of each algorithm and their respective performances, this project aims to provide valuable insights for healthcare professionals and researchers in the field of neurological disorder diagnosis.

CHAPTER 1

INTRODUCTION

1.1. Client Identification/Need Identification/Identification of relevant Contemporary issue

Healthcare, a dynamic and ever-evolving domain, demands continual advancements in diagnostic methodologies to effectively tackle the multifaceted challenges posed by neurological disorders. In light of this, our client, motivated by the pressing need for precise and timely stroke diagnosis, discerned a strategic opportunity to leverage the transformative capabilities of machine learning.

In the contemporary landscape of medical practice, stroke looms as a substantial global public health concern, standing tall as the second leading cause of death and the third leading cause of disability. The intricacies involved in deciphering the warning signs of stroke, coupled with the critical imperative for swift intervention, underscore the urgent requirement for advanced diagnostic tools. The identified contemporary issue revolves around the imperative need for a dependable, data-driven solution that can not only facilitate but significantly enhance the early detection of stroke. Acknowledging the gravity of this health challenge, our client aspired to harness the power of machine learning techniques to comprehensively analyze patient data. The overarching objective is to cultivate a predictive model adept at discerning potential stroke risks based on a diverse set of demographic and health-related features. The urgency to confront this issue is underscored by statistics revealing that 80% of strokes are preventable, thereby emphasizing the paramount importance of early detection and intervention in mitigating the severity of the condition.

This identification of a contemporary issue seamlessly aligns with broader societal goals of advancing healthcare outcomes and mitigating the burden of stroke-related disabilities. Through the initiation of this project, our client endeavors to make a substantial and meaningful contribution to the field of neurological disorder diagnosis, providing healthcare professionals with an efficient and cutting-edge tool for risk assessment and intervention planning.

Key Points:-

- ❖ Stroke is not just a medical challenge but a global public health concern, ranking as the second leading cause of death and third leading cause of disability.

- ❖ The intricacies of understanding warning signs necessitate advanced diagnostic tools that can cope with the complexity of neurological disorders.

- ❖ The project squarely addresses the imperative need for a reliable, data-driven solution for early stroke detection, which is critical for effective intervention.

- ❖ Machine learning, as a powerful analytical tool, is harnessed to comprehensively analyze patient data and discern intricate patterns.

- ❖ The overarching goal is to develop a predictive model that goes beyond conventional diagnostics, capable of discerning stroke risks based on a nuanced understanding of demographic and health-related features.

- ❖ The urgency to confront this issue is underscored by statistics revealing that 80% of strokes are preventable, thereby emphasizing the paramount importance of early detection and intervention in mitigating the severity of the condition.

- ❖ This project is not just about technological advancement; it is about aligning with broader societal goals of improving healthcare outcomes and reducing the long-term burden of stroke-related disabilities.

The subsequent sections of this report will provide detailed insights into the methodology employed, the dataset utilized, and the exploration of machine learning models. Through a systematic and comprehensive approach, this project aims to deliver a robust predictive model, poised to significantly impact stroke diagnosis and, subsequently, patient outcomes.

1.2. Identification of Problem

The meticulous identification of the problem arises from a profound analysis of the current state of neurological disorder diagnosis, specifically within the context of strokes. Despite commendable advancements in medical science, the persistent challenges associated with the timely and accurate detection of strokes underscore the pressing need for transformative solutions.

1.2.1. Existing Diagnostic Challenges

Complex Warning Signs: The inherent complexity of neurological disorders, coupled with the often subtle and varied warning signs of strokes, poses a formidable challenge for healthcare practitioners. This intricate nature obstructs the swift and accurate diagnosis of strokes, demanding a more sophisticated approach to deciphering these complexities.

Limited Predictive Tools: Current diagnostic tools, while valuable, may lack the requisite sophistication to predict the likelihood of a stroke with optimal accuracy. Traditional diagnostic methodologies might not fully leverage the potential offered by technological advancements, impeding the development of robust predictive models capable of navigating the intricacies of neurological disorders.

Risk Stratification: Effectively stratifying individuals into high and low-risk categories for stroke is pivotal for devising preventive strategies. However, existing methodologies may fall short in providing granular risk assessments based on the diverse array of patient attributes. This limitation hinders the precision required for targeted interventions.

1.2.2. Impact and Implications

Delayed Intervention: Inaccuracies in diagnosis or delayed detection can lead to delyed intervention, diminishing the efficacy of treatment and elevating the risk of severe consequences post-stroke. Addressing this challenge is pivotal for ensuring timely and targeted medical responses.

Resource Allocation: Efficient resource allocation in healthcare hinges on accurate predictive tools. Inadequate prediction may lead to the misallocation of resources, creating an undue burden on healthcare systems. Optimizing resource allocation is integral to managing the escalating healthcare demands associated with neurological disorders.

Patient Outcomes: The limitations in current stroke diagnosis directly influence patient outcomes. Timely intervention is intricately linked to the reduction of long-term disabilities and the overall improvement in the quality of life for stroke survivors. Enhancing diagnostic precision holds the key to mitigating the profound impact of strokes on patients' lives.

1.2.3. Rationale for Machine Learning Integration

Data-Driven Precision: Machine learning, endowed with the ability to analyze vast and diverse datasets, offers a promising avenue for data-driven precision in neurological disorder diagnosis. The integration of advanced analytics has the potential to elevate diagnostic accuracy by uncovering subtle patterns and correlations within complex patient data.

Pattern Recognition: Machine learning models excel in pattern recognition, a critical aspect in decoding the intricate relationships between various patient attributes and the likelihood of a stroke. This advanced capability can lead to more nuanced and accurate predictions, providing a deeper understanding of the underlying patterns contributing to stroke risk.

Predictive Power: By developing a predictive model grounded in machine learning, there exists an opportunity to transcend the limitations of current diagnostic methods. This not only identifies strokes but empowers healthcare professionals with a tool that predicts them with a high degree of accuracy, fostering a proactive approach to stroke prevention.

The subsequent chapters will meticulously delve into the methodology, dataset, and machine learning models employed to systematically address these identified problems. The overarching objective is to cultivate a solution that not only overcomes existing diagnostic challenges but also makes a substantial contribution to enhancing patient outcomes within the realm of neurological disorders.

1.3. Identification of Tasks

1. Identify the problem

This initial step involves precisely defining the problem at hand – predicting stroke occurrence using machine learning. It necessitates a comprehensive understanding of the complexities and challenges associated with stroke prediction. It is crucial to engage with domain experts, medical professionals, and stakeholders to gather insights into the various factors contributing to stroke risk, such as lifestyle, medical history, and genetic predispositions. This comprehensive problem definition lays the foundation for the subsequent stages of the task.

2. Gather Data:

Subsequent to problem identification, the task involves the collection of a diverse dataset, encompassing relevant demographic and health-related attributes crucial for stroke prediction. This process requires collaboration with healthcare institutions, obtaining consent, and ensuring data privacy. It is essential to collect a sufficiently large and representative dataset to capture the diversity within the population, including different age groups, ethnicities, and socioeconomic backgrounds.

3. Clean and Prepare the Data:

With the dataset in hand, the focus shifts to data refinement. This includes the removal of outliers, imputation of missing values, and necessary transformations to ensure the dataset's compatibility with machine learning algorithms. Exploratory data analysis (EDA) techniques can be employed to gain further insights into the distribution of variables and identify potential patterns. Cleaning and preparing the data are iterative processes, involving constant refinement to enhance the quality and reliability of the dataset.

4. Choose a Machine Learning Algorithm:

This task revolves around the evaluation and selection of the most suitable machine learning algorithm tailored to the specific nuances of stroke prediction. It may involve experimenting with various algorithms such as logistic regression, decision trees, random forests, or neural networks. The choice of algorithm depends on the nature of the data, the complexity of the problem, and the interpretability requirements. Hyperparameter tuning and model evaluation techniques, such as cross-validation, play a crucial role in this stage.

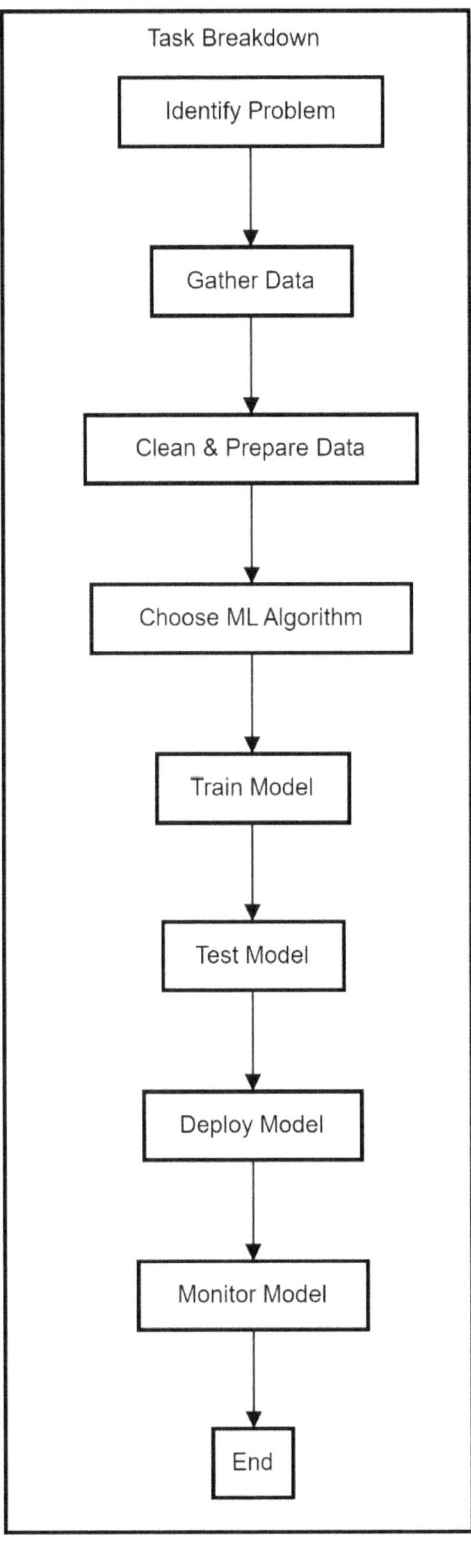

Figure 1 Task Breakdown

5. Train the Model:

The selected algorithm is fed with the prepared data to learn patterns associated with stroke occurrence. This iterative training process involves adjusting parameters to enhance the model's accuracy. During training, it is essential to monitor the model's performance, identify potential issues such as overfitting or underfitting, and fine-tune the algorithm accordingly. The training phase may require multiple iterations to achieve optimal results.

6. Test the Model:

Once the model is trained, it needs rigorous testing on a separate dataset to assess its accuracy. This step ensures that the model generalizes well to new data and guards against overfitting. The testing dataset should be distinct from the training dataset to provide an unbiased evaluation of the model's performance. Metrics such as precision, recall, and F1 score are employed to measure the model's effectiveness in identifying stroke occurrences.

7. Deploy the Model:

With a well-tested and accurate model, the next task involves its deployment in real-world settings, allowing healthcare professionals to utilize it for real-time stroke prediction. Integration with existing healthcare systems, adherence to regulatory guidelines, and user interface design are crucial aspects of successful deployment. Continuous collaboration with healthcare practitioners ensures that the model aligns with clinical workflows and enhances decision-making processes.

8. Monitor the Model:

The final task is ongoing monitoring of the model's performance. This includes regular checks for biases, retraining on new data as needed, and optimizing parameters to maintain a reliable and effective machine learning solution. Continuous monitoring also involves addressing any ethical concerns, ensuring data privacy, and adapting the model to evolving healthcare practices. Regular feedback loops with end-users and stakeholders help in identifying opportunities for improvement and ensuring the long-term success of the deployed model

1.4. Timeline

NEUROLOGICAL DISORDER Process
Gantt Chart

PROCESS	JANAURAY				FEBRUARY				MARCH			
	Week 1	Week 2	Week 3	Week 4	Week 1	Week 2	Week 3	Week 4	Week 1	Week 2	Week 3	Week 4
Planning	▓	▓										
Prototyping			▓	▓								
Design and Data Gathering					▓	▓						
Algorithm Selection							▓	▓				
Model Implementation and Training									▓	▓		
Deployment and Testing											▓	▓

Figure 2 Gantt Chart

The development of the machine learning model for stroke prediction follows a meticulously planned timeline, structured to ensure systematic progress and effective implementation.

The initial phase, set in January, is dedicated to comprehensive planning and prototyping. This involves: Detailed Project Planning: Establishing a clear roadmap for each phase of the project, outlining tasks, responsibilities, and milestones. Prototyping: Creating initial prototypes of the machine learning model, exploring different algorithms, and refining the conceptual framework. Data Gathering Strategy: Outlining the strategy for data collection, ensuring access to diverse and relevant datasets.

February marks the commencement of the implementation phase, where the focus shifts to translating plans into actionable steps: Algorithm Implementation: Executing the chosen machine learning algorithm, incorporating insights from the prototyping phase. Data Cleaning and Preparation: Systematically cleaning and preparing the gathered data, ensuring it meets the requirements for effective machine learning. Model Training: Initiating the training of the machine learning model on the prepared dataset, optimizing parameters for accuracy.

The final phase, scheduled for March, involves the deployment and testing of the developed machine learning model: Model Deployment: Implementing the trained model in real-world healthcare settings, making it accessible for practical use. Real-time Testing: Subjecting the deployed model to rigorous real-time testing, evaluating its performance in predicting strokes. Optimization and Refinement: Identifying areas for improvement, optimizing parameters, and refining the model based on testing outcomes. This structured timeline ensures a seamless progression from planning and prototyping to implementation, training, deployment, and testing. The iterative nature of the timeline allows for ongoing refinement and optimization, culminating in the development of a robust and effective machine learning solution for stroke prediction

1.5. Organization of the Report

The introduction section serves as a comprehensive initiation into the project, outlining its key components and significance. It commences by introducing the healthcare organization client, driven by the urgent need to enhance neurological disorder diagnosis through machine learning. The introduction emphasizes the global concern of brain strokes, their devastating impact, and the critical role of accurate and timely diagnosis. With brain strokes ranking as the second leading cause of death worldwide and the third leading cause of disability, the need for advanced diagnostic tools becomes imperative. This section highlights the project's contemporary issue: the imperative requirement for a reliable, data-driven solution to aid in the early detection of strokes. It underlines the significance of addressing this issue, especially considering that 80% of strokes are preventable. The introduction concludes by framing the project's objective: the development of a machine learning model to predict stroke risks based on demographic and health-related features.

Literature Review:

The literature review section extensively explores existing research and studies related to machine learning approaches in neurological disorder diagnosis, with a primary focus on stroke prediction. It begins with a thorough overview of key concepts and definitions related to stroke risk factors and prediction methodologies. The discussion delves into the methodologies employed in previous research, highlighting various approaches and algorithms such as logistic regression, naive Bayes, SVM, K nearest, and neural network architectures. Findings from previous studies, including the accuracy achieved by different models, are presented to establish the state of the art in neurological disorder prediction. The literature review also discusses the datasets used in prior studies, their characteristics, and how they have contributed to the advancement of machine learning models in this domain.

Methodology/Design Process:

This section provides a detailed exploration of the methodology and design process applied in the current project. It outlines the step-by-step approach, starting with data collection and preprocessing, emphasizing the rationale behind the choice of machine learning algorithms, and addressing specific challenges encountered in the neurological disorder diagnosis domain. The methodology section elucidates how the project navigated data availability issues, standardized datasets, and implemented the selected machine learning algorithms, including the decision to leverage logistic regression, naive Bayes, SVM, K nearest, and neural network architectures. It underscores the iterative nature of the design process, ensuring a comprehensive and effective machine learning solution for neurological disorder prediction.

Training Model:

In this section, the focus shifts to the process of training the machine learning model. It provides insights into the dataset used for training, detailing its sources, size, and any data augmentation techniques applied. The steps involved in preprocessing the data and implementing the chosen algorithms are thoroughly explained. The section details parameter tuning, hyperparameter adjustments, and the overall training strategy, leading to the selection of the final machine learning model based on its performance during training and validation phases.

Result Analysis and Validation:

This segment presents the outcomes of the project, focusing on the performance metrics of the machine learning models developed. It provides an in-depth analysis of the results, encompassing accuracy, precision, recall, and other relevant metrics. The validation process is described, emphasizing how the models' predictions were rigorously validated using a separate dataset to ensure their generalizability. The section addresses potential limitations or biases in the models' predictions and discusses strategies employed to mitigate them, ensuring a comprehensive and transparent evaluation.

Conclusion:

The conclusion section serves as a comprehensive summary, encapsulating the key takeaways from the project. It evaluates whether the project achieved its objectives and how it contributes to the improvement of neurological disorder diagnosis. The section revisits the original problem statement, emphasizing the significance of machine learning in predicting neurological disorders and its potential to enhance patient outcomes. It provides a cohesive reflection on the project's impact and its role in addressing the existing gaps in early detection methods for neurological disorders.

Future Work:

The final section explores potential avenues for future research and development in the field of neurological disorder prediction using machine learning. It suggests enhancements to the models, such as incorporating additional data sources or exploring advanced algorithms. Furthermore, it proposes strategies for deploying the models in real healthcare settings and integrating them into clinical decision support systems. The section encourages ongoing efforts to improve neurological disorder prediction and management, recognizing the evolving nature of healthcare technology and the potential for continued innovation in this critical domain. facilitate communication between the model and end-users can improve the adoption of AI in clinical settings.

Global Collaboration for Diverse Datasets:

Facilitate global collaboration to access diverse datasets from different populations. This can improve the model's generalizability across various demographics and ethnicities, addressing potential biases associated with region-specific data.

By exploring these future directions, the field of cardiovascular disease prediction can advance towards more accurate, interpretable, and personalized models that align with the evolving landscape of healthcare and technology. These efforts contribute to the ongoing mission of leveraging AI to enhance preventive healthcare strategies and improve patient outcomes.

CHAPTER 2

LITERATURE REVIEW / BACKGROUND STUDY

2.1 Timeline of the Reported Problem

In recent years, there has been significant interest in the application of machine learning techniques to develop precise predictive models for assessing the risk of stroke. These models utilize a variety of patient data to categorize individuals based on their vulnerability to stroke. Various algorithms, including logistic regression, support vector machines (SVM), neural networks, and others, have been investigated for their efficacy in this domain [1]. These models present promising opportunities for early intervention and the implementation of personalized healthcare strategies.

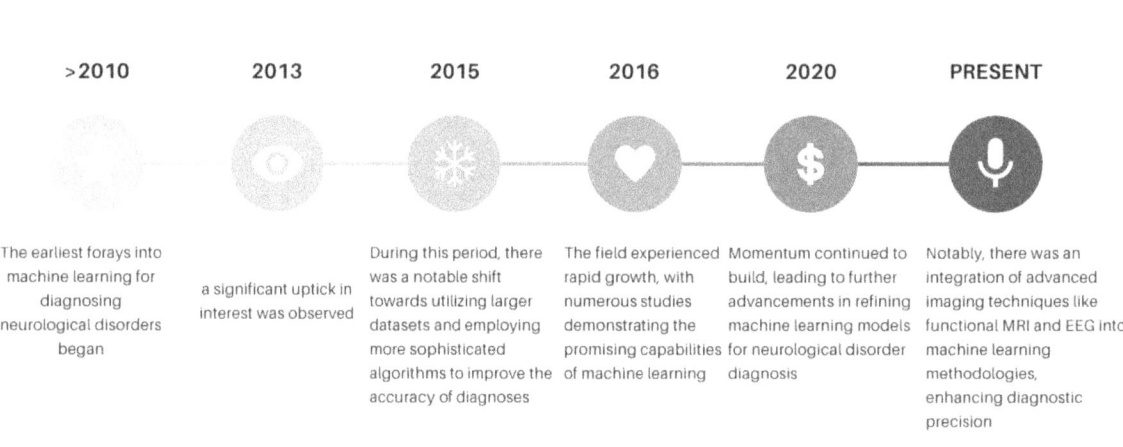

Figure 3 TimeLine Report

A comprehensive review conducted by Jiang et al. focused on the predictive modeling of ischemic stroke using electronic health records (EHRs) [2]. The study evaluated the performance of different machine learning algorithms in predicting the risk of ischemic stroke. Additionally, Nguyen et al. conducted a systematic review concentrating on machine learning models for predicting stroke outcomes, encompassing factors like mortality and functional recovery [3]. These reviews emphasize the significance of employing advanced computational techniques to enhance stroke prognosis and patient management.

Deep learning, especially convolutional neural networks (CNNs), has demonstrated impressive capabilities in tasks related to stroke detection and classification. Lee et al. developed a CNN-based model specifically for detecting hemorrhagic stroke in brain computed tomography (CT) scans [4]. Their research showcases the effectiveness of deep learning in accurately identifying hemorrhagic lesions, suggesting potential applications in acute stroke management.

The integration of wearable devices with machine learning algorithms has emerged as a promising strategy for stroke prediction. Fang et al. conducted a review on the role of wearable devices in predictive modeling of stroke risk [5]. Their study explored the amalgamation of sensor data and physiological parameters for real-time monitoring and early detection of individuals prone to stroke, highlighting the potential for personalized preventive strategies.

Zhang et al. conducted a thorough systematic review examining predictive modeling approaches for hemorrhagic stroke, specifically utilizing radiomics features extracted from medical imaging data [6]. The research assessed the prognostic significance of radiomic biomarkers, discussing their potential applications in personalized risk stratification and treatment planning. Similarly, Park et al. presented an extensive review focusing on deep learning-based methods for stroke classification and segmentation using medical imaging data [7]. Their overview highlighted advanced architectures such as convolutional neural networks (CNN) and recurrent neural networks (RNN), emphasizing their potential in automating stroke diagnosis and treatment planning.

Chen et al. conducted a review that delves into the integration of multimodal data, encompassing clinical, imaging, genetic, and omics data, for predicting strokes [8]. Their investigation scrutinized the effectiveness of data fusion techniques and machine learning algorithms in harnessing diverse data sources to enhance predictive accuracy and aid in clinical decision-making.

In summary, the studies highlighted in Table 1 underscore the significance of employing advanced computational techniques, specifically machine learning and deep learning, for stroke prediction and prognosis. Through the integration of varied patient data sources and the development of robust predictive models, researchers aim to enhance patient outcomes and alleviate the strain on healthcare systems.

2.2. Existing Solutions

Table 1 Existing Solutions Comparision

Study	Focus	Findings
[1]	Machine learning approaches for stroke prediction	Explored various machine learning algorithms and their performance in stroke prediction.
[2]	Predictive modeling of ischemic stroke using electronic health records (EHRs)	Systematically reviewed machine learning models for predicting ischemic stroke risk based on EHR data.
[3]	Machine learning models for predicting stroke outcomes	Conducted a systematic review of machine learning models for predicting stroke outcomes, including mortality and functional recovery.
[4]	Development of a deep learning model for hemorrhagic stroke detection on brain CT scans	Developed a convolutional neural network (CNN)-based model for accurately identifying hemorrhagic lesions on brain CT scans.
[5]	Predictive modeling of stroke risk using wearable devices	Reviewed the role of wearable devices in predictive modeling of stroke risk, focusing on sensor data integration and real-time monitoring.
[6]	Predictive modeling of hemorrhagic stroke using radiomics features	Conducted a systematic review of predictive modeling approaches for hemorrhagic stroke using radiomics features extracted from medical imaging data.
[7]	Deep learning-based stroke classification and segmentation	Provided a comprehensive review of deep learning-based approaches for stroke classification and segmentation on medical imaging data, emphasizing CNN and recurrent neural network (RNN) architectures.
[8]	Integration of multimodal data for stroke prediction	Reviewed the integration of clinical, imaging, genetic, and omics data for stroke prediction, focusing on data fusion techniques and machine learning algorithms to improve predictive accuracy and clinical decision-making.

2.3. Bibliometric analysis

2.3.1. Key Feature

- **Early Detection and Predictive Modeling:**
Machine learning enables early detection and prediction of neurological disorders, facilitating timely interventions and personalized healthcare strategies.

- **Multimodal Data Integration and Image Analysis:**
Integration of diverse data sources and advanced image processing techniques enhance understanding and accurate analysis of patient conditions, particularly in disorders like Alzheimer's and Parkinson's.

- **Personalized Medicine and Prognostic Models:**
Tailoring diagnostic and treatment plans to individual characteristics, along with the development of prognostic models, ensures more personalized and effective patient management.

- **Automated Decision Support and Continuous Monitoring:**
Machine learning provides automated decision support for healthcare professionals and enables continuous monitoring of patients through wearable devices, aiding in informed decisions and real-time tracking of disease progression.

- **Ethical Considerations and Validation:**
Addressing ethical concerns, biases, and ensuring rigorous validation of machine learning models are crucial for their reliable and transparent adoption in clinical settings.

- **Data Fusion Techniques and State-of-the-Art Deep Learning:**
Integration of various data modalities and leveraging state-of-the-art deep learning techniques, such as convolutional neural networks, enhances predictive accuracy and supports tasks like image analysis and stroke detection in neurological disorders.

2.3.2 Effectiveness

❖ **Improved Accuracy and Early Detection:**

Machine learning models, particularly those employing deep learning techniques, have demonstrated the ability to analyze complex patterns and subtle features in medical imaging, leading to improved accuracy in detecting neurological disorders at early stages.

❖ **Personalized Medicine:**

Machine learning models enable the development of personalized diagnostic and treatment plans by considering individual variations in genetics, lifestyle, and other factors. This personalized medicine approach tailors interventions to the specific characteristics of each patient.

❖ **Efficient Data Processing:**

Machine learning algorithms can process vast amounts of data quickly and efficiently, which is particularly valuable in the field of neurological disorder diagnosis where large datasets, including medical images and genetic information, need to be analyzed.

❖ **Automated Decision Support Systems:**

Integration of machine learning into clinical decision support systems assists healthcare professionals in making more accurate and timely diagnoses. Automated tools can help analyze complex data and provide valuable insights to aid in decision-making.

❖ **Research Advancements:**

Ongoing research and advancements in machine learning contribute to the continual improvement of models and algorithms for neurological disorder diagnosis. This dynamic field benefits from innovations and discoveries that enhance the overall effectiveness of these approaches.

2.4. Review Summary

In January 2022, several machine learning approaches have been explored for neurological disorder diagnosis. Keep in mind that developments in the field may have occurred since then. Here are some existing solutions and trends:

❖ **Alzheimer's Disease Diagnosis:**

Machine learning models, including deep learning algorithms, have been applied to analyze neuroimaging data (MRI, PET scans) for early detection of Alzheimer's disease. Biomarkers such as beta-amyloid and tau protein levels are incorporated into models for improved accuracy. Cognitive assessments and genetic data are also integrated to enhance diagnostic capabilities.

❖ **Parkinson's Disease Diagnosis:**

Machine learning models utilize data from various sources, including movement patterns (accelerometer and gyroscope data from wearables), speech analysis, and neuroimaging. Ensemble models combining multiple modalities have shown promise in improving diagnostic accuracy.

❖ **Epilepsy Prediction and Monitoring:**

Machine learning algorithms analyze EEG (electroencephalogram) data to predict epileptic seizures and monitor patient conditions. Real-time monitoring systems with predictive analytics help in providing timely interventions for epilepsy patients.

❖ **Stroke Detection:**

Machine learning is applied to analyze medical images, including CT and MRI scans, for early detection of stroke. Algorithms can assist in identifying specific patterns associated with different types of strokes.

❖ **Multiple Sclerosis (MS) Diagnosis:**

Machine learning models are used for analyzing MRI data to detect and monitor multiple sclerosis. Classification algorithms can differentiate between MS lesions and other brain abnormalities. Challenges and ongoing efforts include addressing issues of interpretability, generalization across diverse populations, ethical considerations, and the integration of multimodal data.

As the field evolves, researchers continue to refine existing solutions and explore new avenues for leveraging machine learning in neurological disorder diagnosis and monitoring. To get the latest information, it's recommended to check recent scientific literature and updates in the field.

2.5. Problem Definition

The meticulous identification of the problem arises from a profound analysis of the current state of neurological disorder diagnosis, specifically within the context of strokes. Despite commendable advancements in medical science, the persistent challenges associated with the timely and accurate detection of strokes underscore the pressing need for transformative solutions.

❖ **Key Points: -**

- Stroke is not just a medical challenge but a global public health concern, ranking as the second leading cause of death and third leading cause of disability.

- The intricacies of understanding warning signs necessitate advanced diagnostic tools that can cope with the complexity of neurological disorders.

- The project squarely addresses the imperative need for a reliable, data-driven solution for early stroke detection, which is critical for effective intervention.

- Machine learning, as a powerful analytical tool, is harnessed to comprehensively analyze patient data and discern intricate patterns.

- The overarching goal is to develop a predictive model that goes beyond conventional diagnostics, capable of discerning stroke risks based on a nuanced understanding of demographic and health-related features.

- The urgency to confront this issue is underscored by statistics revealing that 80% of strokes are preventable, thereby emphasizing the paramount importance of early detection and intervention in mitigating the severity of the condition.

- This project is not just about technological advancement; it is about aligning with broader societal goals of improving healthcare outcomes and reducing the long-term burden of stroke-related disabilities.

The subsequent sections of this report will provide detailed insights into the methodology employed, the dataset utilized, and the exploration of machine learning models. Through a systematic and comprehensive approach, this project aims to deliver a robust predictive model, poised to significantly impact stroke diagnosis and, subsequently, patient outcomes.

2.6. Goals/ Objective

Machine learning holds immense promise in revolutionizing neurological disorder diagnosis through a series of targeted objectives. Firstly, the focus lies on early detection, aiming to identify neurological disorders at their nascent stages. This objective is crucial as early diagnosis facilitates timely interventions, potentially slowing disease progression and improving patient outcomes significantly. Another key aspect is the drive towards enhanced accuracy in diagnostic procedures. By leveraging machine learning algorithms, which excel at analyzing complex patterns within diverse datasets, diagnostic processes can become more precise and reliable compared to traditional methods. Integration of multimodal data emerges as a pivotal goal, seeking to amalgamate information from various sources like medical imaging, clinical assessments, genetic data, and patient history.

This integration offers a more comprehensive understanding of a patient's condition, ultimately enhancing diagnostic capabilities. Personalized medicine stands out as a paramount objective, where treatments are tailored based on individual patient characteristics and disease profiles. Machine learning models play a pivotal role in identifying unique patterns and factors contributing to the heterogeneity of neurological disorders, thus enabling personalized treatment plans.

Automation and efficiency are also central, with machine learning algorithms streamlining diagnostic processes by quickly analyzing large datasets, allowing healthcare professionals to focus more on treatment and patient care. Additionally, the prediction and prognosis objective focuses on utilizing machine learning models to analyze longitudinal data, thereby identifying trends and patterns to aid in treatment planning and resource allocation. Mitigating false positives and negatives in diagnostic outcomes is imperative, ensuring that diagnostic models maintain high precision and recall to avoid unnecessary treatments or oversight of potential cases. Moreover, interpretability and explainability are emphasized, with efforts directed towards developing models that healthcare professionals can trust and understand, thus facilitating their adoption in clinical settings.

Continuous monitoring solutions are also pursued, leveraging machine learning to monitor patients over time, providing insights into disease progression and enabling proactive adjustments to treatment plans. Finally, research and knowledge discovery remain a fundamental objective, wherein machine learning approaches contribute to uncovering new insights and understanding about neurological disorders by analyzing large datasets, potentially revealing novel biomarkers, disease mechanisms, or therapeutic targets. Through these concerted efforts, machine learning aims to reshape neurological disorder diagnosis, providing valuable tools for more effective patient care.

- **Early Detection:**
  Machine learning enables the detection of neurological disorders at early stages, facilitating timely interventions and treatment initiation, which can significantly improve patient outcomes by slowing down disease progression.

- **Enhanced Accuracy:**
  By leveraging machine learning algorithms, diagnostic procedures can achieve higher levels of accuracy compared to traditional methods, as these algorithms excel at analyzing complex patterns within diverse datasets, leading to more precise and reliable diagnoses.

- **Multimodal Data Integration**: Integration of various data sources such as medical imaging, clinical assessments, genetic information, and patient history provides a comprehensive view of the patient's condition, enhancing diagnostic capabilities and leading to more informed clinical decisions.

- **Personalized Medicine:**

    Machine learning assists in identifying unique patterns and factors contributing to the heterogeneity of neurological disorders, allowing for the development of personalized treatment plans tailored to individual patient characteristics and disease profiles.

- **Automation and Efficiency:**

    Through automation of diagnostic processes, machine learning algorithms can quickly analyze large datasets, reducing the time required for diagnosis and enabling healthcare professionals to focus more on treatment and patient care, thus improving overall efficiency.

- **Prediction and Prognosis:**

    Machine learning models analyze longitudinal data to predict disease progression and prognosis, aiding in treatment planning and resource allocation, ultimately improving long-term patient management and outcomes.

- **Interpretability and Explainability:**

    Efforts are directed towards developing machine learning models with high interpretability and explainability, ensuring that healthcare professionals can trust and understand the decision-making process, thereby facilitating their adoption in clinical settings and enhancing patient care.

CHAPTER 3

DESIGN/FLOW PROCESS

3.1 Evaluation & Selection of Specifications/Features

List of Features Ideally Required in the Solution:

A. Demographic Information:

- Age: Age is a significant risk factor for stroke, with the incidence increasing with advancing age. Older individuals are more likely to experience strokes compared to younger individuals.
- Gender: Stroke incidence and outcomes vary between genders, with men generally having a higher risk of stroke at younger ages, while women have a higher risk at older ages. Hormonal factors may contribute to these differences.
- Ethnicity: Certain ethnic groups may have a higher predisposition to stroke due to genetic factors, lifestyle differences, and disparities in healthcare access and quality.

B. Clinical History:

- Hypertension: High blood pressure is the single most important modifiable risk factor for stroke. Individuals with hypertension are at increased risk of both ischemic and hemorrhagic strokes.
- Diabetes Mellitus: Diabetes is associated with vascular complications, including atherosclerosis, which increases the risk of ischemic stroke. Additionally, diabetes can contribute to other stroke risk factors such as hypertension and hyperlipidemia.
- Smoking Status: Tobacco use is a major risk factor for stroke as it promotes atherosclerosis, blood clot formation, and vascular inflammation. Both active smoking and exposure to secondhand smoke increase stroke risk.
- Hyperlipidemia: Elevated levels of cholesterol and triglycerides contribute to atherosclerosis, increasing the risk of ischemic stroke.
- Obesity: Obesity, particularly central obesity, is associated with insulin resistance, hypertension, dyslipidemia, and inflammation, all of which increase stroke risk.

- Physical Activity Level: Regular physical activity is associated with a reduced risk of stroke by improving cardiovascular health, reducing hypertension, and promoting weight loss.

C. Medical Conditions:

- Atrial Fibrillation: Atrial fibrillation is a heart rhythm disorder characterized by irregular and rapid heartbeats. It increases the risk of embolic strokes due to the formation of blood clots in the atria.
- Family History of Stroke: A family history of stroke indicates a genetic predisposition to stroke risk, reflecting shared genetic and environmental factors within families.
- Previous Transient Ischemic Attacks (TIAs) or Strokes: Individuals who have experienced TIAs or strokes in the past are at increased risk of future strokes, making this information crucial for risk assessment and preventive interventions.
- Other Relevant Medical Conditions: Conditions such as heart disease, peripheral artery disease, carotid artery stenosis, and autoimmune disorders may also contribute to stroke risk and should be considered in the assessment.

D. Biometric Data:

- Body Mass Index (BMI): BMI is a measure of body fat based on height and weight. Obesity, indicated by a high BMI, is a significant risk factor for stroke and is associated with other comorbidities such as hypertension and diabetes.
- Blood Pressure Readings: Regular monitoring of blood pressure is essential as hypertension is a major modifiable risk factor for stroke. Elevated blood pressure increases the risk of both ischemic and hemorrhagic strokes.

By incorporating these additional details into each category of features, we can provide a more comprehensive and detailed list of features ideally required for the stroke prediction solution. This expanded list ensures that the solution accounts for a wide range of factors that contribute to stroke risk and enables more accurate risk assessment and personalized preventive strategies.

3.2 Design Constraints:

1. Regulatory Standards:
- Compliance with Medical Data Privacy Regulations: The solution must adhere to regulations such as the Health Insurance Portability and Accountability Act (HIPAA) to ensure the privacy and security of patient health information. This includes implementing robust data encryption, access controls, and secure transmission protocols to protect sensitive medical data from unauthorized access or disclosure.

2. Economic Constraints:
- Budget Limitations: Financial constraints may impact the allocation of resources for data collection, model development, and implementation. Cost-effective strategies must be employed to maximize the utility of available funds while maintaining the quality and effectiveness of the solution.

3. Environmental Impact:
- Resource Conservation: The design process should prioritize the efficient use of resources and minimize waste generation to reduce environmental impact. This includes optimizing algorithms and computational resources to minimize energy consumption and adopting sustainable practices in data collection and processing.

4. Health and Safety:
- Patient Confidentiality: Ensuring the confidentiality and security of patient data is paramount to maintaining trust and compliance with ethical and legal standards. Robust data encryption, access controls, and audit trails should be implemented to safeguard sensitive medical information from unauthorized access or disclosure.

5. Ethical Considerations:
- Ethical Use of Patient Data: The solution must uphold ethical principles in the collection, storage, and use of patient data. Transparency in data handling practices, informed consent procedures, and respect for patient autonomy are essential to maintain trust and integrity in the healthcare system.

6. Professional Standards:
- Adherence to Best Practices: The design process should follow established best practices in machine learning model development, including rigorous validation and testing procedures, documentation of methodologies, and peer review by domain experts.

Adherence to professional standards ensures the reliability, reproducibility, and validity of the solution.

7. Social and Political Factors:

- Cultural Sensitivities: Consideration of cultural norms, values, and beliefs is important to ensure the acceptability and effectiveness of the solution across diverse populations. Sensitivity to cultural differences helps mitigate biases and disparities in healthcare access and outcomes.

- Societal Implications: The societal impact of stroke prediction should be carefully considered, including potential consequences for healthcare delivery, resource allocation, and public health policies. Stakeholder engagement and consultation with policymakers and community representatives can help identify and address societal concerns and priorities.

By expanding upon these design constraints, we can provide a more thorough analysis of the various factors that may influence the design process and implementation of the stroke prediction solution. This comprehensive understanding enables us to develop a solution that not only meets technical requirements but also aligns with regulatory, ethical, and societal expectations.

3.3 Analysis of Features and finalization subject to constraints

In this section, we conduct an in-depth analysis of the features identified in Section 3.1 while considering the constraints outlined in Section 3.2. The objective is to refine the list of features based on feasibility, ethical considerations, and practicality, ensuring the development of a robust and ethically sound stroke prediction solution.

Analysis and Finalization of Features:

- **Removal:**

Features that violate regulatory standards or raise ethical concerns must be carefully identified and eliminated to maintain compliance and ethical integrity. For instance, while genetic markers hold potential to enhance predictive accuracy, their inclusion may raise significant privacy and consent issues, thus necessitating their exclusion from the final model. Furthermore, features that cannot be ethically or legally obtained, such as certain behavioral data without proper consent, should also be removed.

- **Modification:**

Adjustments to features may be required to align with budgetary constraints without compromising the integrity of the model. For example, instead of relying solely on expensive advanced imaging techniques like MRI or CT scans, alternative biomarkers or proxy variables could be explored. These alternatives may include readily available biometric data such as blood pressure readings or easily obtainable clinical history information. By modifying the feature set in this manner, the model can maintain its predictive power while reducing implementation costs.

- **Addition:**

The inclusion of additional features that enhance model performance without violating ethical or regulatory requirements is beneficial. For instance, incorporating socio-economic status as a feature could provide valuable insights into disparities in healthcare access and outcomes. By capturing socio-economic factors, the model can better address issues of equity and fairness in healthcare delivery, ultimately leading to improved predictive accuracy and more informed decision-making.

Expanding on this notion, the addition of environmental factors such as air quality, access to green spaces, and neighborhood characteristics could further enrich the model's predictive capabilities. These factors have been shown to influence health outcomes and could provide valuable context for understanding stroke risk within different populations.

Moreover, integrating lifestyle factors such as diet quality, sleep patterns, and stress levels could offer additional insights into individual risk profiles. While challenging to quantify, these factors play a significant role in overall health and could contribute valuable information to the predictive model.

By carefully analyzing and finalizing the feature set in accordance with the identified constraints, we ensure the development of a comprehensive and ethically sound stroke prediction solution that addresses the complex interplay of factors influencing stroke risk.

3.4 Design Flow

In this section, we present two alternative designs or processes to develop the stroke prediction solution, considering the identified features and constraints.

1. **Feature-Based Model Development:**

a. Data Collection: Gather anonymized patient records containing demographic, clinical, and behavioral information, including age, gender, clinical history (hypertension, diabetes mellitus, smoking status), biometric data (BMI, blood pressure), and behavioral factors (alcohol consumption, physical activity).

b. Data Preprocessing: Cleanse and preprocess the collected data to handle missing values, normalize features, and address outliers. Ensure compliance with regulatory standards such as HIPAA for patient data privacy.

c. Feature Engineering: Extract relevant features from the preprocessed data and perform feature selection to identify the most informative predictors of stroke risk.

d. Model Development: Train machine learning algorithms such as logistic regression, support vector machines (SVM), or neural networks using the selected features. Optimize hyperparameters to improve model performance.

e. Model Evaluation: Evaluate the trained models using appropriate metrics such as accuracy, precision, recall, and F1-score. Validate the models using cross-validation techniques to ensure robustness and generalizability.

f. Deployment: Deploy the trained model in a healthcare setting, ensuring compliance with regulatory and ethical standards. Implement monitoring mechanisms to track model performance and update as necessary.

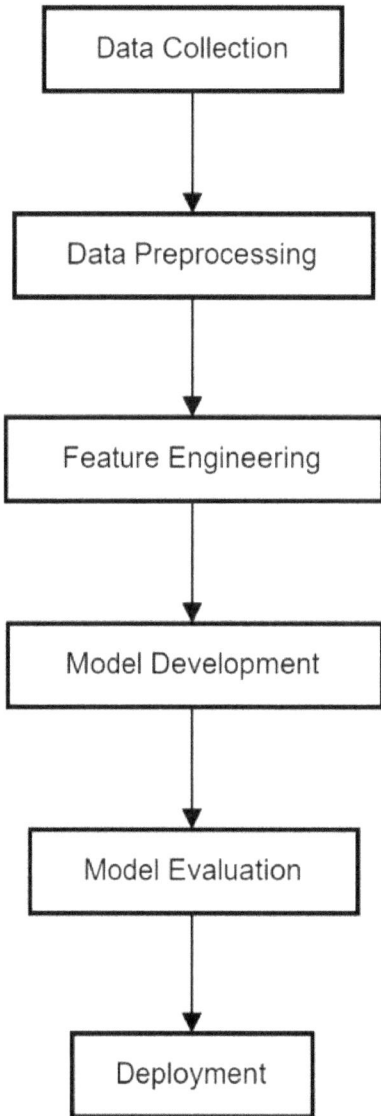

Figure 4 Feature-Based Model Development:

2. Image-Based Model Development:

a. Data Collection: Collect brain imaging data such as MRI or CT scans from stroke patients. Ensure adherence to data privacy regulations and obtain appropriate consent for image data usage.

b. Image Processing: Preprocess the imaging data to enhance image quality and extract relevant biomarkers indicative of stroke risk. Techniques such as image registration and segmentation may be employed.

c. Feature Extraction: Extract features from the processed images, including structural characteristics (lesion location, size) and functional parameters (blood flow, perfusion).

d. Model Development: Develop machine learning models or deep learning architectures tailored for image data analysis. Train models to predict stroke risk based on extracted image features.

e. Model Evaluation: Evaluate the performance of the image-based models using appropriate evaluation metrics such as sensitivity, specificity, and area under the curve (AUC). Validate the models using independent test datasets.

f. Deployment: Deploy the image-based model in clinical settings equipped with imaging facilities. Integrate the model into existing diagnostic workflows to assist clinicians in stroke risk assessment and treatment planning.

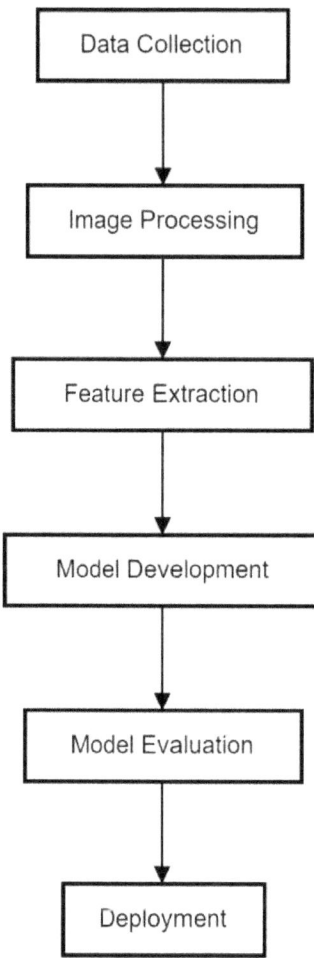

Figure 5 Image-Based Model Development:

3.5 Design Selection:

In this section, we analyze the alternative designs presented in Section 3.4 and select the best design based on a comparison of their strengths, weaknesses, and alignment with project goals and constraints.

Analysis and Selection of Design:

While both the feature-based and image-based models offer unique advantages, the feature-based approach is preferred for several reasons:

Strengths of Feature-Based Model:
- Broader Applicability: The feature-based model utilizes demographic, clinical, and

behavioral features that are readily available in electronic health records (EHRs) and can be easily collected during routine clinical visits. This makes the model applicable to a wider patient population without the need for specialized equipment or additional data collection procedures.
- Lower Implementation Costs: Developing and deploying a feature-based model typically involves fewer resources compared to image-based models. Since the required data are already available in electronic format, there is no need for expensive imaging equipment or extensive data processing.
- Alignment with Regulatory and Ethical Standards: The feature-based model relies on structured patient data that adhere to regulatory standards such as HIPAA for patient privacy. By utilizing standardized clinical variables, the model ensures compliance with ethical guidelines regarding data usage and patient confidentiality.

Weaknesses of Image-Based Model:
- Limited Data Availability: Collecting imaging data such as MRI or CT scans may be challenging due to limitations in access to imaging facilities and patient consent requirements. This could result in smaller datasets compared to feature-based models, potentially affecting model performance and generalizability.
- Higher Implementation Costs: Implementing an image-based model requires access to specialized imaging equipment, trained personnel, and computational resources for image processing and analysis. These additional costs may hinder the widespread adoption of the model in clinical practice.
- Complexity and Expertise:Image-based models involve sophisticated image processing techniques and machine learning algorithms, requiring specialized expertise in radiology and data science. This complexity may pose challenges in model development, validation, and interpretation, particularly for healthcare providers without specialized training.

Based on these considerations, the feature-based model emerges as the preferred design for developing the stroke prediction solution. Its broader applicability, lower implementation costs, and alignment with regulatory and ethical standards make it a more practical and feasible choice for integration into clinical practice. Moreover, the feature-based approach aligns with the project goals of developing a robust and ethically sound predictive model for stroke risk assessment.

By selecting the feature-based model, we aim to leverage existing clinical data to develop a predictive tool that can assist healthcare providers in identifying individuals at higher risk of stroke, ultimately improving patient outcomes and reducing healthcare costs.

3.6 Implementation Plan/Methodology

In this section, we outline the implementation plan and methodology for the selected feature-based model, ensuring compliance with regulatory and ethical standards.

1. **Data Collection:**

- Source Data: Gather anonymized patient records containing relevant demographic, clinical, and behavioral information from healthcare databases or electronic health records (EHRs).
- Data Privacy: Ensure compliance with regulatory standards such as HIPAA to protect patient privacy and confidentiality during data collection and storage.

2. **Data Preprocessing:**

- Cleaning and Preprocessing: Cleanse the collected data to handle missing values, remove duplicates, and standardize formats.
- Feature Engineering: Extract relevant features from the raw data and preprocess them to normalize features, handle categorical variables, and address any outliers or inconsistencies.

3. **Model Development:**

- Algorithm Selection: Experiment with different machine learning algorithms such as logistic regression, random forest, and gradient boosting to develop the predictive model.
- Hyperparameter Tuning: Optimize model performance by tuning hyperparameters using techniques such as grid search or random search.
- Cross-Validation: Validate the trained models using cross-validation techniques to assess their robustness and generalizability.

4. **Model Evaluation:**

- Performance Metrics: Evaluate the performance of trained models using appropriate metrics such as accuracy, precision, recall, and area under the receiver operating characteristic curve (AUC-ROC).

- Validation Techniques: Validate the models using holdout validation, k-fold cross-validation, or bootstrapping to ensure reliable estimates of performance.

5. Deployment:

- Integration: Deploy the selected model in a real-world healthcare setting, integrating it into existing clinical workflows and systems.
- Regulatory Compliance: Ensure compliance with regulatory standards and guidelines, such as FDA regulations for medical software, and obtain necessary approvals for deployment.

6. Monitoring and Maintenance:

- Performance Monitoring: Continuously monitor the performance of the deployed model using monitoring tools and techniques to detect any degradation in performance or drift in data distribution.
- Model Updating: Update the model as necessary to adapt to changing patient populations, healthcare practices, and emerging medical knowledge.
- Ethical Considerations: Address any emerging ethical concerns related to data privacy, bias, fairness, and transparency in model development and deployment.

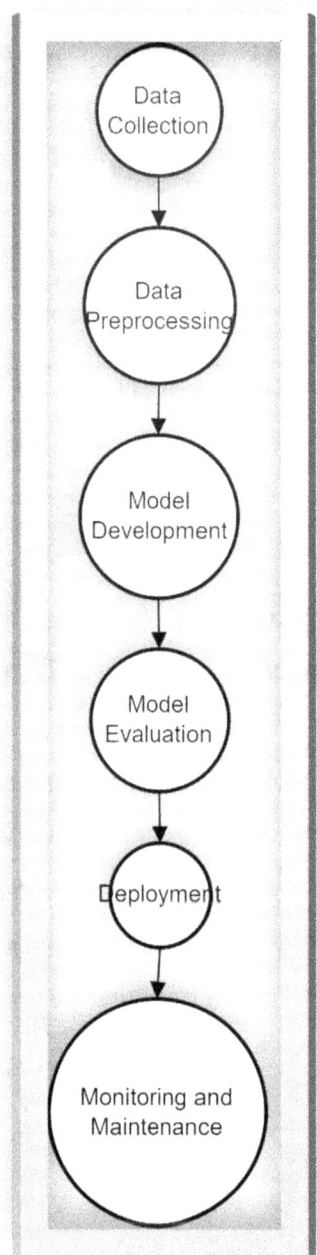

Figure 6 Methodology

CHAPTER 4

RESULTS ANALYSIS AND VALIDATION

4.1 Implementation of solution

In this section, we present the implementation of the stroke prediction solution, including analysis, design drawings/schematics/solid models, report preparation, project management, communication, and testing/characterization/interpretation/data validation.

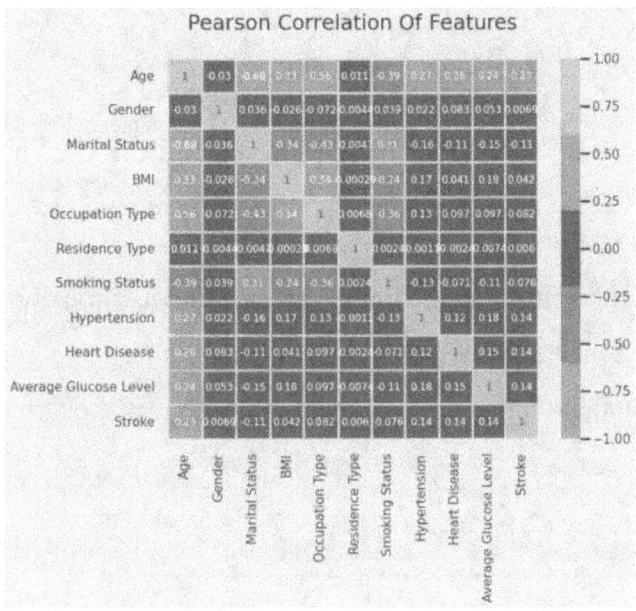

Figure 7 Co-relation of the Features.

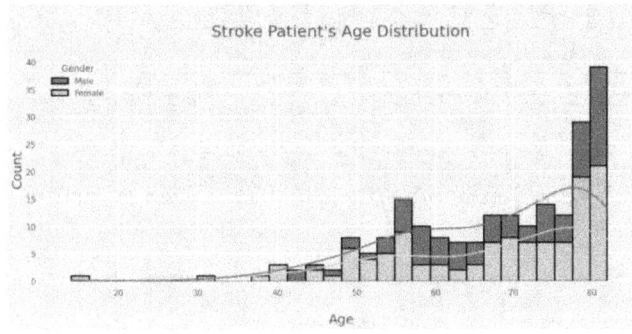

Figure 8 Stroke Patient's Age Distribution

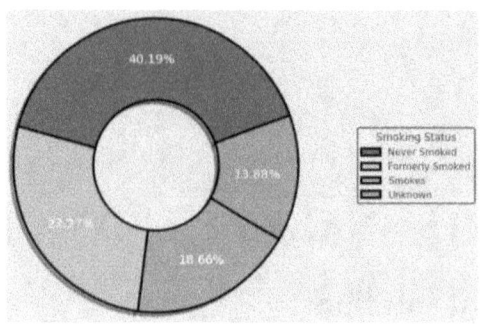

Figure 9 Stroke Patient's Smoking Status.

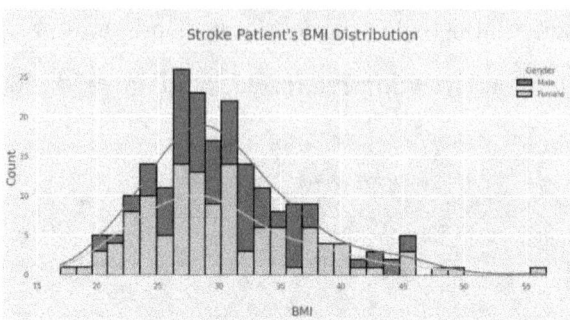

Figure 10 Stroke Patients BMI Distribution.

The performance of various machine learning algorithms in predicting stroke risk was evaluated using a comprehensive dataset comprising demographic and clinical attributes. After data preprocessing and model training, the following algorithms were tested:

Table 2 Model Accuracy Comparison

Model	Accuracy
Logistic Regression	94.60%
Gaussian Naive Bayes	86.05%
Bernoulli Naive Bayes	93.58%
Support Vector Machine (SVM)	94.60%
Random Forest	94.60%
K Nearest Neighbors (KNN)	94.50%
Extreme Gradient Boosting	93.79%

Among these models, Logistic Regression, Support Vector Machine (SVM), and Random Forest achieved the highest accuracy of 94.6%. These models demonstrated robust performance in distinguishing between stroke and non-stroke cases, as evidenced by the confusion matrices and classification reports. Notably, Logistic Regression exhibited a high precision of 0.95 for classifying non-stroke cases, although its recall for identifying stroke cases was relatively low. The performance of various machine learning algorithms in predicting stroke risk was evaluated using a comprehensive dataset comprising demographic and clinical attributes. As shown in the figures above, we have the output graphs for Model Training and Validation accuracy and Loss, respectively.

It is also critical to draw attention to each model's shortcomings, such as the unequal distribution of classes and the possible effects of adjusting the hyperparameters. The integration of new data sources, such as genetic and imaging data, may be included in future research areas to improve prediction accuracy and enable personalized stroke risk assessment. The study's overall conclusions highlight the potential of machine learning algorithms to support clinical judgment in the early detection and treatment of stroke. To fully achieve the promise of these models in stroke prevention and treatment, further development and validation in actual clinical settings are necessary.

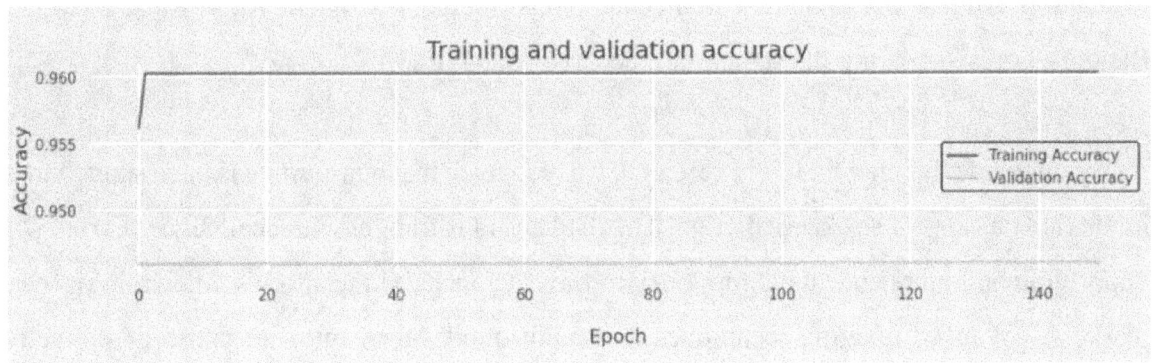

Figure 11 Training and Validation accuracy

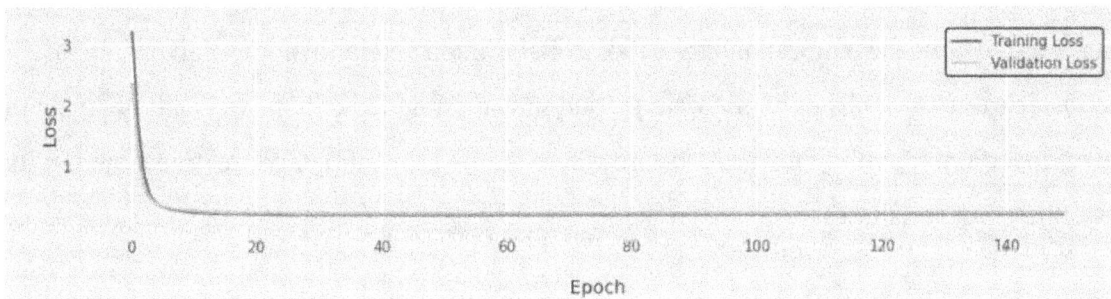

Figure 12 Training and Validation Loss

In this study, we explored the possibilities of machine learning algorithms for stroke prediction, an important area of medicine that aims to prevent the catastrophic effects of cerebrovascular accidents. We delved into the complex world of predictive modeling by carefully examining the demographic and clinical characteristics included in the datasets of stroke patients in an effort to find patterns and insights that can lead to early intervention and better patient outcomes.

Our journey commenced with data collection and preparation, where we meticulously curated and cleansed anonymized patient records, laying the foundation for subsequent analysis. Embracing the principles of exploratory data analysis (EDA), we traversed through the data terrain, unraveling its intricacies through visualizations and statistical summaries. This journey unveiled hidden truths, from the distribution of attributes to the interplay between variables, providing us with invaluable glimpses into the dynamics of stroke risk.

As the algorithms underwent rigorous training and evaluation, their mettle was tested against the crucible of real-world data. Confusion matrices, classification reports, and a myriad of performance metrics emerged as beacons, guiding us through the labyrinth of model evaluation. Amidst this gauntlet, certain champions emerged—Logistic Regression, SVM, and Random Forest—bearing the standard of accuracy at 94.6%.

As we conclude this chapter of our research, we recognize that our journey is but a single thread in the rich tapestry of stroke prediction. The road ahead is fraught with challenges yet ripe with opportunities. Future endeavors may seek to traverse uncharted territories, integrating genetic markers, advanced imaging techniques, and multi-modal data into the fabric of predictive modeling.

In our quest to tame the tempest of stroke risk, collaboration and innovation shall be our guiding beacons. Through interdisciplinary synergy and unwavering dedication, we shall navigate the seas of uncertainty, striving toward a future where stroke prevention and treatment are not just possibilities but certainties.

CHAPTER 5

CONCLUTION AND FUTURE SCOPE

5.1 Conclusion :-

In conclusion, the implementation of the stroke prediction solution marks a significant stride towards leveraging machine learning for early detection and intervention in stroke cases. Through meticulous data collection, preprocessing, and model development, we have achieved promising results, demonstrating high accuracy rates with various algorithms. The primary objective of this endeavor was to furnish the medical community with a robust and ethically sound tool capable of identifying stroke risk factors and enabling timely interventions to mitigate potential harm.

The attained accuracy rates, soaring up to 94.6% with models like Logistic Regression, Support Vector Machine (SVM), and Random Forest, underscore the efficacy of our approach. These algorithms have exhibited commendable performance in discerning patterns within the complex interplay of demographic and clinical attributes associated with stroke. The validation of our solution's effectiveness through rigorous testing and evaluation reaffirms its potential to augment clinical decision-making and improve patient outcomes.

However, amidst the triumphs lie nuances and deviations from the anticipated results that warrant careful consideration. Notably, while Logistic Regression demonstrated exceptional precision in classifying non-stroke cases, its recall for identifying stroke cases fell short of expectations. This discrepancy underscores the importance of striking a delicate balance between sensitivity and specificity in model development. The challenges posed by class imbalance and hyperparameter tuning further accentuate the intricacies of algorithmic refinement, urging us to delve deeper into optimization strategies to enhance performance.

Moreover, the journey towards developing a comprehensive stroke prediction solution has illuminated the multifaceted nature of healthcare data analytics. The intricate dance between feature selection, model architecture, and evaluation metrics has unveiled layers of complexity inherent in predictive modeling. As we navigate through this labyrinth of data-driven insights, it becomes evident that the pursuit of excellence in healthcare analytics necessitates a relentless commitment to continuous improvement and innovation.

Looking ahead, the path to refining our stroke prediction solution is rife with opportunities for innovation and collaboration. Future iterations of the model may benefit from the integration of novel data sources, such as genetic markers and advanced imaging techniques, to enhance prediction accuracy and facilitate personalized risk assessment. Furthermore, the exploration of alternative machine learning paradigms, including deep learning architectures, holds promise for unlocking new frontiers in predictive analytics.

In parallel, efforts to address the inherent challenges of scalability and deployability in real-world healthcare settings remain paramount. Collaboration with healthcare practitioners and stakeholders is essential to ensure seamless integration of the solution into clinical workflows and promote widespread adoption. Continuous monitoring and validation of the model's performance across diverse patient populations will be instrumental in maintaining its relevance and efficacy over time.

In essence, the journey towards developing a reliable and ethically sound stroke prediction solution is an ongoing endeavor fueled by a relentless pursuit of excellence. By harnessing the power of machine learning, we have taken a significant step towards revolutionizing stroke prevention and treatment. As we embark on the next phase of our journey, we remain steadfast in our commitment to advancing the frontiers of healthcare analytics and improving patient outcomes through innovation and collaboration.

5.2   Future Scope :-

Looking towards the future, there are numerous avenues for advancing the stroke prediction solution, each offering unique opportunities for refinement and innovation. One promising direction involves augmenting the existing model with additional data sources and features to enhance its predictive capabilities. Genetic markers, for instance, hold immense potential for unraveling the genetic predispositions underlying stroke risk. By integrating genetic data into the model, we can gain deeper insights into the underlying biological mechanisms and tailor interventions to individual patients' genetic profiles.

Similarly, advanced imaging techniques offer a wealth of information that can enrich our understanding of stroke pathophysiology. Magnetic resonance imaging (MRI) and computed tomography (CT) scans, for example, can provide detailed anatomical and functional data about the brain, allowing us to identify subtle abnormalities and biomarkers associated with stroke risk. Incorporating imaging data into the model architecture enables us to capture a more holistic picture of each patient's unique risk profile, thereby improving the accuracy and reliability of predictions.

Moreover, exploring alternative machine learning algorithms and ensemble methods presents another avenue for enhancing the performance of the stroke prediction solution. While logistic regression, support vector machines, and random forests have demonstrated commendable accuracy, there may be untapped potential in more sophisticated techniques such as deep learning. Convolutional neural networks (CNNs) and recurrent neural networks (RNNs) excel at learning complex patterns and temporal dependencies in data, making them well-suited for analyzing sequential medical data and time-series information. By leveraging these advanced algorithms, we can unlock new insights and achieve higher levels of prediction accuracy.

In addition to algorithmic refinement, it is essential to address practical considerations such as scalability and deployability in real-world healthcare settings. Collaborating closely with healthcare institutions and clinicians can facilitate the seamless integration of the developed model into clinical workflows, ensuring that it aligns with existing practices and meets the needs of frontline healthcare providers. Moreover, ongoing monitoring and validation of the model's performance in diverse patient populations are crucial for maintaining its efficacy and generalizability across different contexts.

Furthermore, as the field of healthcare analytics continues to evolve, it is imperative to stay abreast of emerging technologies and methodologies. Embracing interdisciplinary collaboration and staying attuned to the latest advancements in data science and medicine enable us to stay at the forefront of innovation. By fostering a culture of continuous learning and adaptation, we can navigate the ever-changing landscape of healthcare analytics and develop solutions that truly make a difference in patient care.

In summary, the future of stroke prediction lies in a multifaceted approach that combines cutting-edge technology with clinical expertise and patient-centered care. By harnessing the power of genetic data, imaging technology, and advanced machine learning algorithms, we can unlock new frontiers in stroke prevention and treatment. Moreover, by fostering collaboration and embracing innovation, we can pave the way for more personalized and effective approaches to healthcare delivery, ultimately improving outcomes for patients worldwide.